Let's Discover Canada
QUEBEC

by
Suzanne LeVert

George Sheppard
McMaster University
General Editor

Produced by The Philip Lief Group, Inc.

CHELSEA HOUSE PUBLISHERS
New York   Philadelphia

On the cover:

A fisherman on the Gaspé
Peninsula stands in front of one
of Quebec's most remarkable
landmarks, Percé Rock.

DESIGN: Allen Design
PROJECT EDITOR: Suzanne LeVert
EDITOR: Robyn M. Feller
PICTURE RESEARCHER: Joan Beard

First printing

1   3   5   7   9   8   6   4   2

Library of Congress Cataloging-in-Publication Data

LeVert, Suzanne
  Let's Discover Canada. Quebec/by Suzanne LeVert; George Sheppard, general editor. p. cm.
  "Produced by The Philip Lief Group, Inc."
  Includes bibliographical references.
  Summary: Discusses the geographical, historical, and cultural aspects of Canada's largest province.
Includes maps, illustrated fact spreads, and other illustrations.
  ISBN 0-7910-1030-9
  1. Quebec (Province)—Juvenile literature. 1. Quebec (Province) I. Suzanne LeVert. Title.
F1052.4.L48 1991
971.4—dc20

Contents

My Canada

by Pierre Berton

"Nobody knows my country," a great Canadian journalist, Bruce Hutchison, wrote almost half a century ago. It is still true. Most Americans, I think, see Canada as a pleasant vacationland and not much more. And yet we are the United States's greatest single commercial customer, and the United States is our largest customer.

Lacking a major movie industry, we have made no wide screen epics to chronicle our triumphs and our tragedies. But then there has been little blood in our colonial past—no revolutions, no civil war, not even a wild west. Yet our history is crammed with remarkable men and women. I'm thinking of Joshua Slocum, the first man to sail alone around the world, and Robert Henderson, the prospector who helped start the Klondike gold rush. I'm thinking of some of our famous artists and writers—comedian Dan Aykroyd, novelists Margaret Atwood and Robertson Davies, such popular performers as Michael J. Fox, Anne Murray, Gordon Lightfoot, and k.d. lang, and hockey greats from Maurice Richard to Gordie Howe to Wayne Gretzky.

The real shape of Canada explains why our greatest epic has been the building of the Pacific Railway to unite the nation fromsea to sea in

1885. On the map, the country looks square. But because the over-whelming majority of Canadians live within 100 miles of the U.S. bor-der, in practical terms the nation is long and skinny. We are in fact an archipelago of population islands separated by implacable barriers—the angry ocean, three mountain walls, and the Canadian Shield, that vast desert of billion-year-old rock that sprawls over half the country, rich in mineral treasures, impossible for agriculture.

Canada's geography makes the country difficult to govern and explains our obsession with transportation and communication. The government has to be involved in railways, airlines, and broadcasting networks as it is involved with social services such as universal medical care. Rugged individualism is not a Canadian quality. Given the envi-ronment, people long ago learned to work together for security.

It is ironic that the very bulwarks that separate us—the chiseled peaks of the Selkirk Mountains, the gnarled scarps north of Lake Superior, the ice-choked waters of Northumberland Strait—should also be among our greatest attractions for tourists and artists. But if that is the paradox of Canada, it is also the glory.

A lighthouse and a church steeple form a typical landscape on the Gaspé Peninsula.

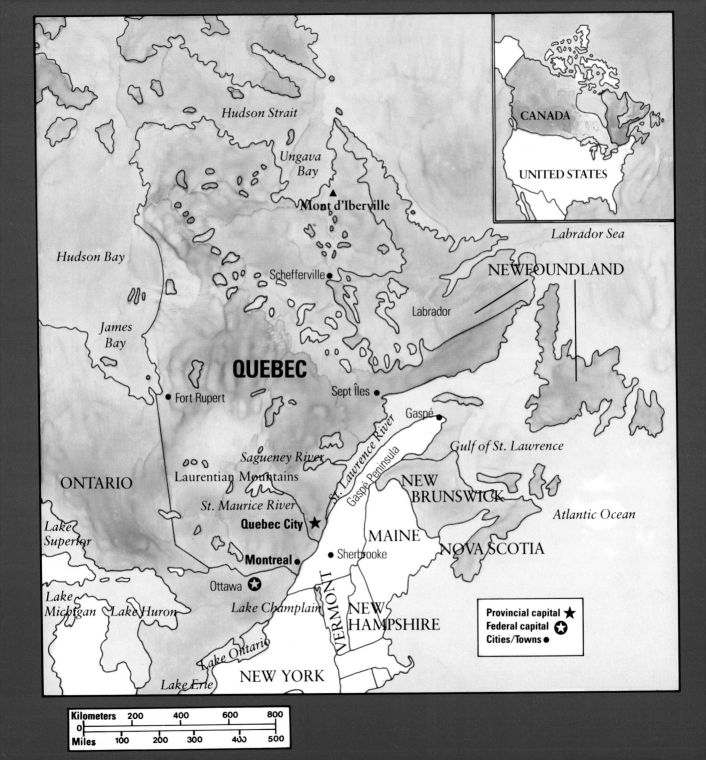

Madonna Lily

Snowy Owl

Quebec at a Glance

Population: 6.5 million
Area: 594,860 sq. miles
(1.5 million sq. km)
Capital: Quebec City
Largest City: Montreal
Flag: adopted January 21, 1948
Flower: madonna lily, adopted 1963
Bird: snowy owl, adopted 1897
Coat of arms: adopted in 1608

Government: parliamentary system; one-house legislature called the National Assembly of Quebec. Made up of 108 members elected by popular vote by district for terms. The province's chief executive officer, the premier, is the head of the ruling party.
Major industries: pulp and paper products, food processing, automobile manufacture
Motto: *Je me souviens*; "I remember"

The Land

The largest province in Canada, Quebec is the main bastion of French culture and language in North America. Its vast natural resources, dynamic politics, and rich history combine with its French traditions to make it one of the most unique and vital communities in all of North America.

Covering approximately 595,000 square miles (1.5 million sq. km), Quebec could fit within its borders all of Spain, Portugal, France, Belgium, and both East and West Germany. Twice the size of the state of Texas, Quebec has a varied topography and an intensely beautiful landscape. More than 16 percent of the world's fresh water is found in this province's myriad lakes and rivers. Altogether Quebec has some 5,000 miles (8,000 km) of coastline, and its inland waters cover some 71,000 square miles (184,000 sq. km) of territory.

Bordered on the south by four American states (Vermont, New Hampshire, Maine, and New York), on the west by Ontario, on the east by New Brunswick and Labrador (a part of the province of Newfoundland), and on the north by James and Hudson bays, Quebec's central location on the St. Lawrence River has contributed to its prominent role in Canadian history.

The Vallée de la Pimbina, *opposite,* in the heart of the Laurentian Mountains is just one example of Quebec's natural beauty. Today, the Laurentians include one of the most popular skiing and camping areas in the province.
Above, the Gaspé Peninsula is one of the earth's oldest lands regions; Percé Rock, shown here, is embedded with many fossils.

Quebec is composed of three major geological regions. The Canadian Shield, comprising almost half of Canada's terrain, covers more than 80 percent of Quebec. An area of ancient rock forming a vast plateau of lakes, rivers, and forests, the Canadian or Pre-Cambrian Shield is a vast, horseshoe-shaped region. Through the ages, most of the Shield's soil was scraped away by glaciers, wind, and water, leaving much of it rocky and infertile. However, the Shield does contain rich deposits of valuable minerals, including gold, copper, and iron ore.

Mont d'Iberville, at 5,300 feet (1,526 meters) Quebec's highest point, represents the Shield's northeastern border in the province. A mountain chain, the Laurentians, forms its southeastern edge. Within the Shield's borders are contained both the stark, treeless northern tundra and the lush forests (some of the most dense in the country) of the southeast.

In 1970, Ile d'Orléans, located about 40 miles (65 km) from Quebec City, was designated a historical district, officially recognizing the area's century-old homes, churches, and chapels.

The beautiful Eastern Townships, where British loyalists from the United States first made their home, form one of Quebec's most historic regions.

The agricultural heart of the province is the St. Lawrence Lowland, a flat plain made up of rich soil and sand. A small region in the southeast, the Lowland was formed by the waters that flooded the area after the ancient glaciers melted some 13,000 years ago. Lying less than 500 feet (150 meters) above sea level, the Lowland region is dominated by the Monteregian Hills, a series of eight mountains, five of which are more than 1,000 feet (300 meters) high. The best known of these hills is Mont Royal, which overlooks the city of Montreal.

Most important to the development of the Lowland region is its location on the St. Lawrence River. Home to the province's first settlers, the Lowland remains the most populated region in Quebec.

The Appalachian Highlands, south of the St. Lawrence River and bordering the northeastern United States, consists of small mountain formations intersected by fertile farmland. Covering three sections of Quebec—the Gaspé Peninsula, the South Shore, and the Eastern Townships—the Appalachian region has an abundance of stock and dairy farms, apple orchards, and the world's largest deposits of the valuable mineral asbestos.

Waterways

Of all the Canadian provinces, Quebec contains the largest area of inland water. In fact, the territory covered by its more than 1 million lakes and rivers represents an area larger than half of France.

The St. Lawrence River is the province's principal waterway and undoubtedly its most important geographical feature. Flowing over 2,280 miles (3,699 km), the St. Lawrence ranks among the world's greatest rivers. When the St. Lawrence Seaway, connecting the Great Lakes with the Atlantic Ocean, was completed in 1959, the river's

position as Quebec's central transportation artery was further enhanced. The Ottawa River, one of the northern rivers known as tributaries that flow into the St. Lawrence, forms the boundary between Quebec and Ontario. Other important tributaries include the St. Maurice, Saguenay, Richelieu, and St. Francis rivers.

Another important watershed in Quebec is the area around Hudson and James bays. Eight of Quebec's 19 major rivers flow into these bays. Because of its abundance of water, this region has become one of the province's most important sources of hydroelectricity.

Of all the Canadian provinces, Quebec contains the largest area of inland water. Its lakes and rivers, such as this one in the Gatineau Hills, cover about 71 square miles (184,000 sq. km) of territory.

Climate and Regions

Living in Quebec has always meant coming to terms with nature—more specifically, the long, cold, snowy winters common throughout the province. Neither the Canadian Shield nor the Appalachian Mountains provide Quebec with adequate protection against frigid northern air currents.

Even in the southern regions, the weather can be quite severe during the winter months. Snow can be found on Montreal's streets for about 12 weeks every winter, with temperatures averaging about 9 degrees F (− 16 C) in January. The summers in the south, however, do tend to be fairly mild, with an average temperature of about 54 degrees to 68 degrees F (12 degrees to 20 degrees C) in July.

Outdoor winter sports, such as snowshoeing, are popular among Quebec residents.

This snow-covered town is located in Coeur-du-Québec, a region situated halfway between Montreal and Quebec City. Quebec winters are long and hard; even in the south, snow covers the land for nearly four months each year.

The arctic north, on the other hand, is a different matter altogether. In the white silence of the north, fewer than 80 days per year are frost-free; the average temperature on a day in January is 3 degrees F (−23 C) and, in the "heat" of midsummer, just 43 degrees F (11 C).

It might be said, however, that the beauty of Quebec's landscape, its rich resources, and its resourceful people more than make up for its difficult climate. The northern tundra, for instance, is home to about 5,200 Inuit (known as Eskimos to the European settlers), who live in 15 villages scattered along the shores of James Bay, Hudson Bay, Hudson Strait, and Ungava Bay. Although the Inuit no longer live in igloos (instead preferring wood or concrete prefabricated houses), they still earn their livelihood by fishing and hunting. Dwarf birches and lichen are the only plants that can stand the intense cold, but caribou, polar bear, and fox are hearty enough to join the Inuit in this arctic land.

Fishing remains one of Quebec's
vital industries, especially on the
Gaspé Peninsula, where salmon,
bass, and trout abound.

The farther south one travels, the more populated and forested the province becomes. Southern Quebec is home to far more than 90 percent of the province's total population. Most people live in or around Quebec's two largest cities, Montreal and Quebec City, but there are a host of other thriving communities.

The Gaspé Peninsula, for instance, lies east of the St. Lawrence River and has some 200,000 residents. Since Jacques Cartier first arrived here in 1534, Gaspé has been a vital fishing community. More recently, copper mining and forestry have added to its economy. Its landscape is striking, with the Chic-Choc Mountains running down the center of the peninsula and stony beaches dotted with fishing villages decorating its coastline.

The Saguenay region in the middle of the province is marked by powerful rivers and dense forests—some of the densest in the country. Some of the largest hydroelectric plants and pulp and paper mills in the world are located here. In fact, the city of Trois-Rivières, just south of Saguenay, is known as the World's Newsprint Capital because of its productive paper mills.

The Eastern Townships region is one of rolling hills and beautiful lakes. The heart of Quebec's modest agricultural sector, the Eastern Townships also have a number of asbestos mines and textile factories and a thriving tourist industry. The region is known for its rich history as well. The first British settlers— Loyalists who fled the United States during and after the American Revolution—made the Eastern Townships their home.

The frozen tundra of the north, the rugged seacoast of the Gaspé Peninsula, the dense forest of the Saguenay, and the rolling hills and lush farmland of the Eastern Townships are representative of the beauty and diversity of Quebec's remarkable landscape.

The History

It was a 35-year-old Frenchman, the explorer Jacques Cartier, who became the first European to set foot in the province that is now Quebec. In search of a route to China, Cartier landed at Gaspé Peninsula in 1534. Planting a cross and the royal flag, he claimed the land for King Francis I and named it New France.

Cartier made a second trip a year later, again looking for a way to reach the Orient or, if not that, then gold or other riches. Instead, he found another most valuable resource, the mighty St. Lawrence River. Sailing down it, he arrived at Stadacona, an Indian village, on the site of today's Quebec City. The village was perched on the cliffs overlooking a *kebec*, the Stadacona word for "narrowing of the waters." The name Quebec would later be applied to the whole province. Sailing further upstream, Cartier and his crew came upon Hochelaga, a village of about 1,000 Indians, which was to become the city of Montreal.

When Cartier first arrived in New France, the land was inhabited by three major groups of native Americans—the Inuit, the Naskapi, and the Iroquois—as well as significant numbers of Algonquin, Huron, Malecite, and Micmac. The Inuit lived in the far north, chiefly

Named after the first man to set foot on Canadian soil, the Vallée de Jacques Cartier, *opposite*, is a testimony to Quebec's vast water and timber resources. *Above*, Jacques Cartier was just 35 years old when he arrived to claim what is now Quebec for the king of France.

west of Ungava Bay and along the shores of Hudson Bay. The Naskapi hunted in what is now eastern Quebec; members of this tribe who lived toward the south, between the St. Maurice River and present-day Sept-Îles, were called Montagnais-Naskapi (mountain men-Naskapi) by the French.

The Iroquois group, which included the Seneca, Cayuga, Oneida, Onondaga, and Mohawk communities, lived in the area south of the St. Lawrence River and east of the Richelieu River. The Iroquois would prove to be formidable enemies of the French settlers who began arriving in the early 1600s. For well over 50 years, wars between the Iroquois and the French would rage until, in 1701, a treaty between them was signed.

Cartier spent a difficult winter at Cap-Rouge, a few miles upriver of Stadacona, during his next expedition to New France in 1541-42. Finding neither gold nor pleasant living conditions in this bitterly cold, snowy land, Cartier returned to France, leaving no settlers behind. It was not until 66 years later that the settlement of New France really began.

A Tale of Two Cities

In many ways, the story of Quebec can be told by exploring the histories of its two most important cities, Quebec and Montreal. The great explorer Samuel de Champlain arrived in the village of Quebec in 1608 determined to build a French settlement in the land that Cartier had claimed as New France. Beneath the cliffs, which Cartier had dubbed Cap Diamant because he mistakenly thought they contained diamonds, a small group of settlers began to build what would become the center of French Canada. Sturdy walls, the first of the city's many fortifications, were built to protect a trading post and several homes.

It was from Quebec City, strategically located on the St. Lawrence River, that the French launched their commercial enterprises. The city quickly became the economic center of New France, where the fur trade was conducted and where the rugged *coureurs de bois* (woods runners) brought the beaver pelts they had trapped or traded for during their intrepid journeys into the far reaches of New France.

Montreal, on the other hand, was founded as a religious center. In May 1642, Paul de Chomeday de Maisonneuve, a military officer, landed with about 40 settlers, most of them Catholic missionaries. Maisonneuve named the settlement Ville-Marie de Montréal, later shortened to Montreal.

Quebec City in the 18th century was not yet the bustling metropolis it is today, but its many churches and forts and its busy port made it one of early Canada's most important cities.

QUEBEC

A. Le Fort
B. les Recollets
C. La plate forme
D. Les Jesuittes
E. La Cathedralle
F. Le Seminaire
G. l'Hostel Dieu
H. L'éveché
I. La Redoute
K. Le magasin apoudre

Quebec's first bishop, François de Laval, founded Laval University, now one of Canada's most important colleges.

Indeed, religion was central to the colonists' lives in Montreal and Quebec, playing a vital role in the settlement of New France. In the early 17th century, Roman Catholic orders were the first to establish hospitals, schools, and churches. Maisonneuve's group in Montreal included two remarkable Frenchwomen, Jeanne Mance and Marguerite Bourgeoys, whose presence helped to develop the tiny settlement into a thriving community. Jeanne Mance founded Canada's first hospital in Montreal in 1645, and Marguerite Bourgeoys founded the Congregation of Notre-Dame and established a school for girls and young women.

Another important religious leader of the 1600s was François de Laval, the first bishop of Quebec, who arrived in the province in 1659. In 1663, he founded the Séminaire de Québec as a theological college. It has since become Laval University, one of the largest, most prominent colleges in Canada. Laval was named bishop of Quebec in 1674.

The early days of provincial settlement were difficult. In spite of hardship from weather, war, and pestilence, however, the courageous settlers survived. Slowly but surely, their numbers grew. By 1666, the population had reached nearly 3,500. Some were *coureurs de bois*, in search of furs and other valuable commodities. Others worked as missionaries, hoping to convert the native population to Christianity. Still others were explorers—men like René-Robert de La Salle, Pierre d'Iberville, and Louis Joliet—who mapped the North American continent.

Yet not all citizens of New France were missionaries, *coureurs de bois*, or intrepid explorers. On the contrary, many were simple farmers hoping to make a new life for themselves and their families in New France. Known as *habitants*, these permanent settlers were allotted land according to a complex system of land distribution, known as the seigneurial (manorial) system, established in 1627.

The seigneurial system was based on the feudal system and was intended to promote permanent settlement of New France in an organized and productive way. The king of France had granted ownership of New France's land to a company in Quebec, which then distributed the land in lots (known as seigneuries) to wealthy, influential colonists. These landowners or seigneurs then leased the land to farmers, the

A French soldier, circa 1722, clad in typical French Canadian dress, including the essential snowshoes needed for Quebec's long winters.

habitants, who worked the land in exchange for paying rent and taxes to the landowners.

Another system brought to New France from the mother country was the civil code of law. Based on Roman law, civil law sets forth a rigid set of rights and obligations that do not change. The British legal system, on the other hand, is based on common law, which is more fluid and adaptable to the opinions of government, society, and individual judges and courts. A judge in the common law system, for instance, can decide a case on its individual merits, taking into consideration particular circumstances, previous rulings on similar cases, and prevailing public sentiment. Civil law requires judgment to be based strictly on a written, codified body of law, leaving no room for review of similar cases or the opinions of the judge. French Canadians would struggle throughout their history to maintain the civil law system.

The British and the French

It was not long before the French settlers were fighting not only the elements and the Iroquois but also the British. Eager to expand their territories, European powers battled to control the Americas. Wars between the English and French colonies raged constantly during the late 17th and the 18th centuries.

New France was especially hard hit. In 1690, William Phips, a British soldier from Massachusetts, tried to attack Quebec City but was rather handily turned away by Governor Frontenac. In 1711, another British attack on the city was hindered by a storm on the St. Lawrence. But in June 1759, Major General James Wolfe laid the heavily fortified Quebec City under a four-month siege. When French commander Louis-Joseph Montcalm took his troops outside the city to fight on the Plains of Abraham, Wolfe's 8,500 better-trained troops outmaneuvered Montcalm's 3,000 soldiers and 12,000 armed citizens. The battle was bloody, however, and it left both commanders mortally wounded.

A year later, when Montreal fell, the British completed their takeover of New France. Some of New France's elite went back home, leaving the 65,000 French settlers to live under British rule. The struggle to maintain their French identity and heritage had begun.

James Wolfe, a general in the English army, commanded the troops that conquered New France in 1759, bringing it under British rule.

Although Quebec's involvement in the War of 1812 was minimal, an important battle between the United States and England was fought on Lake Champlain, part of the border between Quebec and the United States.

At first, perhaps because the British were by then hearing the drumbeats of rebellion from their American colonies to the south, the French were treated rather kindly by their conquerors. The Quebec Act, written in 1774, allowed the French to keep their language, their legal system, and—much to the distress of the Protestant colonies—their Roman Catholic religion. At the same time, the Act reinstated some territory to the province that the American colonies were hoping to acquire, adding even more fuel to the revolutionary fire. The Quebec Act, in fact, was one of the main causes of the American War of Independence.

Even in 1879, Quebec was a place for festivals and fun. Here, a sleigh race takes place on Montreal's frozen streets.

When the war did begin, one of the earliest campaigns against the British took place in Quebec City in 1775. American troops, led by General Richard Montgomery, first took control of Montreal and then moved northeast where, with the help of the infamous General Benedict Arnold, they hoped to take Quebec City. At the same time, a group of American delegates, including statesman Benjamin Franklin, attempted to convince the French in the province, the *Québecois*, to join their fight against the British. When the Québecois decided against that course of action, a new chapter was added to French Canada's history: Not only would the Québecois struggle against the British to retain their identity, but they would fight against being assimilated by their increasingly powerful southern neighbor, the United States.

In 1791, the Constitutional Act divided what had been New

France into two provinces, Upper Canada (Ontario) and Lower Canada (Quebec). Although this constitution protected Quebec's religion and language, it did nothing to change the fact that the British controlled the economy and had all the political power.

In 1837, a series of violent revolts against the British, led by Louis-Joseph Papineau, took place. Lacking arms and effective leadership, the rebellions were quickly crushed by British troops, but the sentiments voiced would long echo in Quebec and throughout Canada. Later, in 1840, another constitutional act would rename the provinces Canada East (Quebec) and Canada West (Ontario).

The Dominion of Canada

The nation of Canada, as we know it today, was essentially created by the British North America Act of 1867. Four colonies, Canada East (Quebec), Canada West (Ontario), New Brunswick, and Nova Scotia, were united as the Dominion of Canada. Lower Canada, now with a population of about 1.2 million, took back its original name, Quebec.

The system of government in the new Dominion was based largely on the parliamentary system of Great Britain. Each province would have its own government, elected by the general population. In addition, the people would elect representatives to the central, federal government.

The British North America Act recognized both French and English as Quebec's two official languages. It also gave the province direct control over education and civil law. In 1867, Pierre-J.-O. Chauveau became the first premier of Quebec.

French Canadians resented British rule in Canada from the time it began in 1763. Although the federal system that was established in 1867 and the rights it granted the French Canadians partly satisfied them, tension between the British and the French continued to exist.

The Québecois were, in essence, second-class citizens in a province in which they were the vast majority. Their church leaders only made the problem worse, often protecting their own power and influence by siding with the British. The traditional, agrarian values espoused by the Roman Catholic church and its educational

One of Quebec's most internationally famous and domestically popular politicians is Pierre Trudeau, who served as Canada's prime minister from 1968 to 1979 and then again from 1980 to 1984.

institutions would also hold back the French Canadians during industrialization.

Modernization and Industrialization

At the time of confederation, Quebec was a relatively poor province with just over a million people. The next 100 years would see it change dramatically, transforming it from a small, agrarian community to one of Canada's most economically and culturally dynamic provinces.

The process would be a long and difficult one, however. The first step was for Quebec to acquire more territory and resources. In 1912, it nearly doubled its size when its northwest boundaries were extended to Hudson Bay and Hudson Strait. Interest in the region's natural resources grew while Quebec and Newfoundland disputed the Quebec-Labrador boundary. The British Privy Council settled this question in favor of Newfoundland, a decision still resented in Quebec.

During the early part of the 20th century, some people in Quebec resisted the full force of industrialization. It was not until the 1920s that Quebec's shift from agriculture to manufacturing went into high gear. By 1941, the products from Quebec's factories accounted for about 65 percent of its economy. The cities, especially Montreal, grew enormously. In 1867, Montreal was home to about 60,000 people; by the end of the 1950s its population neared the 1 million mark.

A turning point in Quebec's development came with the Great Depression of the 1930s. In addition to the economic crisis, there was a sharp cry for political power from those who feared that the increasingly powerful federal government would encroach upon their provincial rights. In 1936, Maurice Duplessis, head of the new party Union Nationale, was elected premier, Quebec's highest government office. Except for a five-year break from 1940 to 1945, Duplessis would serve until his death in 1959.

Though the Duplessis administration bolstered the more conservative French Canadian population, it did nothing to help Quebec deal with the problems of rapid urbanization and industrialization. It also was a corrupt administration known for its reliance on patronage, and mired in old alliances between the provincial government, the Catholic church, and business interests.

The Quiet Revolution and Today

When Maurice Duplessis died in 1959, Quebec took the opportunity to modernize—and modernize it did during a decade known as the Quiet Revolution. Everything from its educational system to the government itself went through a thorough overhaul. Economists were hired to devise a comprehensive economic plan. Educational administration was taken away from the Catholic church and more emphasis was placed on teaching science and technical subjects. Social needs became a focal point as health and unemployment insurance plans were enacted. The government itself expanded: Four new departments were created, including two to deal with educational and cultural matters.

These reforms have helped create the modern Quebec, one that is a leading economic and political force in Canada. Now a major trad-

In 1976, the newly elected premier Raymond Bourassa, met with René Levesque, head of the Parti Québecois, to discuss putting forth a referendum calling for Quebec to become an independent, French-speaking nation. The amendment was defeated in a popular vote in 1980.

In 1976, more than 200 Indians from the Native Youth Association protested the building of the James Bay hydroelectric power plant located near reserves in the north of Quebec.

ing partner with the United States, Quebec continues to work to fulfill its potential by using its natural resources more efficiently. Montreal is Quebec's economic heart, with thriving service and manufacturing industries.

The main political division in modern Quebec remains between those who favor strong ties with the federal government and those who want more independence for the province. Some even want to make Quebec a completely independent French-speaking nation. All such calls for independence have failed so far, but this dynamic, often turbulent debate continues.

The struggle over French culture and language has only intensified, though major strides have been made. In 1974, French was made the official language of the province, and in 1977, the Charter of the French Language made the use of French mandatory in law, government, commerce, and business.

Today, Quebec remains a unique and fascinating community—the bastion of French culture and heritage in North America.

The Economy

Quebec, rich in natural resources and with a labor force of highly skilled workers and managers, is perhaps for the first time since the earliest days of its history becoming an economic leader of Canada. According to the Organization for Economic Cooperation and Development (OECD), Quebec's citizens enjoy the ninth highest standard of living in the world.

Throughout much of its history, however, Quebec's economic reality lagged behind its great potential. The British had excluded French Canadians, a vast majority in Quebec, from the managerial class of Quebec's business and industry. When many British left the province, most to settle in Ontario, Quebec's economy faltered because of a lack of able managers and entrepreneurs. Other factors, including early resistance to industrialization by more traditional Catholics and an economic shift westward toward Ontario and beyond, have also held back Quebec's economy.

Since the Quiet Revolution of the 1960s, more and more businesses have thrived with talented, creative French Canadians at their helm. Today, Quebec's trade, especially with the United States, is

High technology has become an important economic sector in Quebec. Plants such as the one pictured *opposite* employ thousands of people. *Above*, new construction of office buildings and residential dwellings, especially in the major cities, is also enjoying a boom in Quebec today.

booming. About 40 percent of the province's total production—from clothing and textiles to transportation equipment—is now exported. Indeed, Quebec is one of the leading forces in today's increasingly global marketplace.

Like many industrialized nations, Quebec has seen its economy shift from traditional industries, such as manufacturing, mining, and forestry, to the financial and service industries. Today more than 70 percent of the workforce is employed in Quebec's government offices, financial institutions, and service-related fields. With an active stock exchange and the headquarters of four chartered banks and three major life insurance companies, Montreal is Quebec's financial center.

Manufacturing is Quebec's next largest economic sector. The St. Lawrence Lowland in Quebec and the adjoining Great Lakes region in Ontario form the industrial heartland of Canada. Quebec's forests, minerals, and hydroelectric power resources have played a large part in the development of manufacturing in the province.

High technology—research and development as well as manufacturing—is enjoying a boom in Quebec. Montreal is home to such leaders in aeronautics and telecommunications as Pratt and Whitney, Canadair, and Northern Telecom. Three of the world's largest engineering consulting firms are Quebec-owned, employing nearly 15,000 people. Computer technology is another important factor in Quebec's economic resurgence; this North American center of French-language and culture is becoming a leader in French-language computer software.

Quebec is Canada's major producer of textiles, aluminum, petroleum products, and railway rolling stock. The manufacturing and construction industries now provide almost 25 percent of Quebec's jobs, the largest employers being paper and pulp producers, textile manufacturers, food processing plants, and mining industries. Others include iron smelting, petroleum refining, and the manufacture of steel products.

Quebec's mining industry also plays a major role in the provincial economy. The mining of iron ore, limestone, copper, zinc, and asbestos contributes about $3 billion to the economy, with almost half of the industry's production exported. An estimated 30 percent of the world's asbestos is produced in Quebec, about $400 million of which is exported.

Located on the banks of the St. Lawrence River, Montreal is Quebec's largest city.

The Saguenay region, located in central Quebec, includes some of the province's most bountiful farmland. Wheat fields, such as the one pictured *above*, and a dynamic forestry industry add to Quebec's economy.

At the turn of the century, a remarkable 65 percent of Quebec's income was based on agricultural production, but that figure has now dwindled to only 4 percent of the province's economy. In an effort to enhance Quebec's agricultural potential, the provincial government passed the Agricultural Land Protection Act of 1978. Today, almost 80 percent of Quebec's food requirements are met by its 40,000 dairy, cattle, and vegetable farms.

Also of major importance are the raising of poultry and hogs and the growing of corn and tobacco. Extensive apple orchards are located near Montreal in the Monteregian Hills area, and a full nine-tenths of Canada's maple sugar and syrup are produced in Quebec.

With more than 360,000 sq. miles (940,000 km) of forests, Quebec has the third-largest area of forestland in Canada, after Ontario and British Columbia. Quebec's bountiful forests yield nearly one-third of Canada's pulp and paper products and have made Quebec the world's leading newsprint producer. In fact, the province of Quebec is the world's second-largest producer of pulp and paper, after the United States.

Despite the province's great economic strides, it still faces a very high unemployment rate (approximately 9.5 percent, almost 2 percent higher than the national average). Reasons for such a high rate include a surplus of workers without usable skills in today's high-tech, service-intensive economy and an increased emphasis on automation in the manufacturing industries, which has led to major plant layoffs. However, with more and more people finishing college (20 percent of the population today compared with about 2 percent in the 1950s), and more of those people majoring in business (about 40 percent of students at the University of Quebec), the province continues its quest for more economic power.

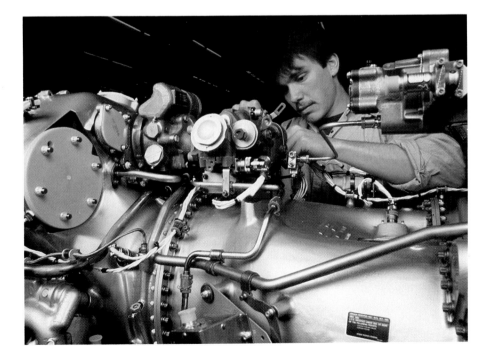

Although many plants have turned to automation, manufacturing still is an important source of employment in Quebec today.

The People

Nearly 6.5 million people now live in the province of Quebec, and almost 5.5 million of them are French speakers. Although this predominance of French language and culture makes Quebec one of the most unique and fascinating communities in North America, it often overshadows one of Quebec's most attractive qualities: a growing ethnic and cultural diversity.

Approximately one-sixth of Quebec's population is English-speaking. Three groups account for the more than 580,000 English speakers in the province; the descendants of the English, Irish, and Scots who came to Quebec after the British conquest of New France; the descendants of colonial Loyalists who arrived at the end of the 18th century; and English-speaking immigrants.

Since 1945, more than half a million people from 80 different nations have decided to make Quebec their home, more than 100,000 since 1981 alone. Most, more than 325,000, came from Europe, but 65,000 people came from Asia and another 33,000 from Africa. Thousands of others, from Latin America, the United States, and the Caribbean, have added their own special customs and traditions to Quebec's mosaic.

Quebec's famous *joie de vivre*, joy of living, is evident in its outdoor cafés and bustling city streets, shown *opposite*. *Above*, during one of Quebec's many festivals, children transform themselves into clowns with the artful use of makeup.

More than 80,000 native Americans live in Quebec today. This family lives in the province's far north, where most of the other 11,000 Inuit, known as Eskimos to Quebec's earliest sellers, also make their home.

However, the "French Fact" is never ignored. Both children and adults who come to live in Quebec are given special introductory French classes. Although some 20 foreign-language newspapers are published in Quebec and several multilingual programs are broadcast on television and radio, the use of French is mandatory in business and government.

Quebec also remains home to more than 80,000 native Americans. This group includes more than 60,000 Indians, 11,000 Metis (people of mixed Indian and European descent), and 7,000 Inuit. Of this number, more than 26,000 live on about 147,000 acres (72,000 ha) of reserved lands set aside for Indians by the federal and provincial governments.

Social Services

Life in Quebec is different than it is anywhere else in Canada, and not just because it is so very French. The way Quebec structures and administers its social services is also quite distinctive.

One of the province's most important pieces of social legislation is its Charter of Human Rights and Freedoms, which recognizes the political, legal, economic, social, and human rights of all Quebec citizens. Under the Charter, which is the most comprehensive in Canada, all people, regardless of race, color, or sex, are treated equally under the law and in the workplace. In addition, a special agency sees to it that children are protected and receive the education and other benefits to which they are entitled.

Publicly funded social services include all levels of education, including universities, most aspects of medicine and health care, special assistance to the poor, and comprehensive programs for the elderly. The government also administers 1,500 hospitals and clinics throughout the province. A comprehensive Consumer Protection Act and a well-established network of day-care centers are other ways the government supports its people.

Education is a top priority. Schools and universities have improved dramatically since the mid-1960s, when Quebec reformed its educational system and attendance increased as a result. With almost 3,000 elementary and secondary schools and about 100 colleges, Quebec has almost 1.5 million adults and children studying in its vast educational network. The University of Quebec, in Quebec City, is the province's largest college, with almost 80,000 students. Montreal University and McGill University, both in Montreal, enroll 56,000 and 27,000 students respectively.

Education is a top priority in Quebec. Nearly 1.5 million children and adults study in the province's 3,100 elementary schools, high schools, and colleges.

Life in Quebec: The Arts and Culture

Today, most of Quebec's population is made up of urban dwellers who live either in Montreal or in Quebec City and their environs. Only five percent live in other regions, such as the Eastern Townships, the Northwest, and the St. Lawrence Lowland, and just 3 percent of today's population live on farms.

Indeed, the density of Quebec's cities makes them particularly exciting. Cosmopolitan and yet with a distinct regard for indigenous culture, the Québecois have an abundance of the special quality called *joie de vivre*, or joy of life. Fine food and good conversation are of supreme importance everywhere in Quebec, but especially in its largest cities.

Music, dance, theater, and the visual arts continue to flourish in Quebec. Since the 1700s, indigenous music has helped to keep Old World traditions and culture alive. In the 1950s and 1960s, Québecois folksingers such as Felix Leclerc, GillesVigneault, and Robert Charlebois brought to life Quebec's unique cultural heritage. Acting as traveling troubadours, these musical artists encouraged a renaissance in French-language popular music that is carried on today by artists such as Claude Léveillée, Jean-Pierre Ferland, and Diane Tell.

Classical music, opera, modern jazz, and rock and roll are extremely popular in Quebec. Montreal and Quebec City both have a number of symphony orchestras and dance companies and host two of the most important jazz festivals in the world. The British rock group The Police and singer-songwriters David Bowie and Cat Stevens are just a few of the many international rock stars who have recorded albums in Quebec's state-of-the-art recording studios.

Quebec also has approximately 10 active theater companies. Each offers at least one new play a year written by a Québecois. Some 80 summer theater companies are scattered throughout Quebec, bringing the excitement of live theater to even the most remote communities.

The visual arts also thrive. Quebec has some 50 museums, including the Musée des Beaux-Arts, the Museum of Quebec and the Museum of Civilization, which show the works of artists both from Quebec and from around the world. Although many of Quebec's early painters followed European artistic trends, the mid-20th century saw

Amateur and professional artists alike use Quebec's city streets and rural landscapes as inspiration for their paintings and photographs.

Canada's favorite sport at its most exciting: the Montreal Canadiens (in red and blue) score a goal against the Toronto Maple Leafs (in white and blue).

the emergence of a movement—first described in the manifesto, *Le Refus global*—calling for the creation of original Quebec art. Painters such as Marc-Aurèle Fortin and Jean-Paul Lemieux, and the sculptors Robert Roussil and Jordi Bonet, brought this manifesto to life in their distinctly French Canadian work.

Quebec's rich literary tradition has blossomed in the late 20th century. Anne Hébert, Mordecai Richler, and Yves Baushemin are just a few of Quebec's most renowned novelists and playwrights. Leonard Cohen, a novelist, poet, and songwriter, is one of Quebec's most internationally known artists.

Leisure Time

At the top of almost every Canadian's favorite hobbies is the sport of hockey, and nowhere is that more true than in Quebec. The province is home to two major league hockey teams, the Montreal Canadiens and the Quebec Nordiques, and Quebec's players are among the best in the world. During the 1950s, 1960s, and 1970s, the Montreal Canadiens, with stars such as Maurice Richard, and Guy Lafleur, were perhaps the most powerful team in hockey's history, winning the National Hockey League's Stanley Cup a total of 16 times. Since then other countries, especially the Soviet Union, have challenged Canadian dominance in the sport, and this has only increased fans' enthusiasm for this exciting game. Baseball follows quick on hockey's heels in terms of popularity—the Montreal Expos draw thousands of fans from across the province.

When not watching or participating in their favorite sports, Québecois enjoy the great outdoors in all its splendor. Winter sports of all kinds are especially popular—there are 95 alpine ski centers within two hours of Montreal and Quebec City. In the summer, Quebec's coastline and lakeshores are cluttered with tourists eager to enjoy the rare warm sun while boating and swimming.

Carrying a small kayak, a tourist takes advantage of Quebec's many opportunities for outdoor adventure.

The Cities

Montreal

With a population of some 3 million people in the greater Montreal region, Montreal is not only the largest city in Quebec but also the second-largest French-speaking city (after Paris) in the world. Canada's second-largest city (after Toronto) is an island 32 miles (51 km) long and more than 10 miles (16 km) across at its widest point. Although the greater Montreal region makes up slightly less than 3 percent of Quebec's total land surface, it is home to more than half the population and 70 percent of Quebec's manufacturing industries.

Indians and Europeans alike settled here because three converging rivers made Montreal a natural communications and transportation center. From here, the fur trade prospered, with *coureurs des bois* sailing past the roiling, unnavigable Lachine rapids to rejoin the St. Lawrence further west and press on to the heart of the continent.

Today, this tradition continues, as Montreal has become one of North America's major business centers. More than two hundred large companies have their head offices in Montreal, and these are joined by new ones every year. These companies currently include 12 banks, 15

The view from Mont Royal, located in Montreal's center, is spectacular, especially at night when the city sparkles, shown *opposite*. *Above*, seeing Quebec City's old-world architecture while riding in a calèche (horse-drawn buggy) is one of the capital city's special pleasures.

major insurance firms, several important brokerage firms, the Stock Exchange, and Canada's three major engineering consultant firms: SNC, Lavalin, and Moneco. These three companies are among the top 15 firms of their kind in the world.

Montreal is also Quebec's main cultural center: jazz, theater, modern dance, ballet, cinema, television, radio, classical music (chamber orchestra and symphony orchestra), opera, museums, publishing houses, and art galleries all thrive here.

There are also three major universities in Montreal—the University of Montreal, the University of Quebec, and McGill University—all of which are internationally recognized for the quality of their teaching and research in a variety of fields, especially bio-technology, telecommunications, and computer science.

From the summit of Mont Royal, located almost in the center of the city, Montreal and the St. Lawrence stretch out as far as the eye can see. With trails criss-crossing its wooded hills and with a lake, Lac des Castors, near its summit, Mont Royal is a favorite with Montrealers seeking relaxation from the hustle and bustle of city life.

A mounted policeman takes a look at Montreal from Mont Royal, which rises 764 feet (233 m) above the city.

An exciting ride spins daring passengers at Man and His World, an amusement park on the site of Montreal's Expo 67, one of North America's largest world fairs.

Another of Montreal's distinctions is its "underground city," a network of passages underneath the city, linking comfortable offices overlooking Mont Royal and the St. Lawrence in the new section of the city with the business buildings of Old Montreal. Lined with shops, restaurants, and galleries, this city-within-a-city attracts thousands of residents and tourists alike.

Recent decades have brought Montreal into the global spotlight. In 1967, the city hosted one of North America's largest world's fairs, Expo 67. More than 50 million people from 70 nations participated during the six-month run, recalled each summer with special events held at the Man and His World site and in the amusement park La Ronde.

The city also hosted the 21st Olympic games in 1976, building a unique "flying saucer" stadium seating 70,000 and a complex that includes a six-pool swimming arena and a velodrome for cycling. The Olympic Park, an impressive sports complex of bold design, is located at the east end of Montreal; in 1987, a retractable roof was added, making the stadium usable during all four seasons of the year. The stadium is home to the Montreal Expos baseball team and regularly hosts gigantic trade shows, rock concerts, and other special events.

More than any other part of this fascinating city, however, it is the cobblestone streets of Old Montreal that most reflect its three centuries of history and its promising future. Montreal—the new and the old—is an exciting, cosmopolitan city, where the night life is as important as the business of the day. Its restaurants are among the best in the world; indeed, many culinary experts consider Montreal to be the gastronomic capital of North America.

Quebec City

With a population of more than half a million people in the Quebec City region (about 165,000 in the city itself), the provincial capital of this French region is a distinctly beautiful city. In fact, the oldest part of Quebec City, known in French as Vieux Québec, was recently declared a world heritage site by UNESCO, the United Nations Educational, Scientific, and Cultural Organization. Its fortress of cobblestone streets and 18th-century architecture, claims UNESCO, makes the city of "outstanding universal value, ranking with Egypt's pyramids and India's Taj Mahal."

The provincial capital, Quebec City, is strategically located on the St. Lawrence River.

With its quaint 18th century archi- tecture, Vieux Québec, the oldest part of Quebec City, was desig- nated a world heritage site by UNESCO, the United Nations Educational, Scientific, and Cultural Organization.

Prior to the arrival of the Europeans, the site of modern Quebec City was occupied by Indian hunters and fishermen for several thousands of years. In 1535, Jacques Cartier discovered a fairly large Iroquoian village he called Stadacona, but sometime between 1543 and 1608, when Samuel de Champlain arrived at the site, the Stadaconans had disappeared and had been replaced by the occasional nomadic Algonquians, likely Naskapi.

Although Quebec City was the capital of the French empire in North America in the early days of New France, it remained little more than a village for more than 200 years. In 1608, it had 28 inhabitants; by the time of the British conquest in 1759–60, its population only slightly exceeded 8,000. It was not until the mid-1800s, when government and economic activities began to concentrate here, that the population began to grow, reaching about 60,000 in 1861.

Quebec City's strategic location on the St. Lawrence River largely determined the nature of its development. In the age of sail, the city held a dominant position as a port of entry and exit for oceangoing vessels. It quickly became the transfer port for domestic and foreign trade, especially furs and timber, and the arrival and departure point for travelers and immigrants to North America. From the beginning, Quebec City's location made it a political, administrative, and military center of the province.

Quebec City's growth was also due to its fortifications; it remains the only walled city in modern North America. Its value as a military fortress was first realized by the founder of New France, Samuel de Champlain. It was Champlain who built Fort St.-Louis in 1620, at the highest point of the cliff known as Cap Diamant. Walls were built around the entire city when the Comte de Frontenac took over the colony's administration in 1672. The fortress often was used to defend the colony against the British, until Quebec fell to General James Wolfe in 1759. Later, fear of attacks by the United States prompted the British to build the Citadel, a giant star-shaped bunker on Cap Diamant.

Today, entering the old, walled city is like passing through a time warp. The walls and great arched gates lead to an area so reminiscent of 17th- and 18th-century France that it is difficult to believe Quebec City is a modern metropolis. Extremely proud of their heritage, the Québecois have preserved dozens of buildings, battle sites, and monuments.

The Citadel, located behind the church to the right, is the largest fort in North America still used as a military base.

But Quebec City is indeed modern. With bustling business and industrial districts, a major port, and a host of theaters and museums, it ranks among the most vibrant cities in all of Canada. As the provincial capital, the city also has political traditions that run strong and deep. The 1791 constitution made Quebec City the capital of Lower Canada, and it remained so until the 1840 Act of Union. The city played an even larger role as the national capital of the United Canadas from 1852 to 1855 and again from 1860 to 1865.

Its present role as capital of the province originated with the Canadian Confederation in 1867, which saw most of the provinces in present-day Canada join together as one country. Today, Quebec's government is the city's largest employer. The 30,000 civil servants who live and work here make up the bulk of its labor force. Many also work in the city's hospitals and educational institutions.

Quebec City remains the major center of French culture and the seat of the only francophone (French-speaking) government in North America. In addition to conserving these traditions, it has managed to maintain a greater cultural homogeneity than Montreal, the other major pole of the French culture. Its teaching institutions include the Séminaire de Québec and Laval University. Until 1920 the latter was the only francophone university in Quebec; its satellite campus in Montreal became the University of Montreal in 1920.

The historical character of Quebec City is reflected in the architecture of the old city, which has been the subject of major restorations and has become the site of exceptional museums. The municipal, provincial, and federal governments have combined their efforts to restore Place Royale, Artillery Park and the fortifications of the Old Port, the Musée du Séminaire, and the Museum of Civilization. The Museum of Quebec contains collections of ancient and modern artworks and is part of a large urban park, the Plains of Abraham or Parc des Champs de Bataille, which commemorates the battle leading to the fall of the city and of New France to the British army in 1759. There is also a zoological garden in Orsainville, north of the city, an aquarium near the Pont de Quebec, and the Grand Theatre de Quebec, home to the Quebec Symphony Orchestra.

Things to Do and See

• **Montreal Botanical Gardens,** Montreal: The third largest in the world, with more than 25,000 different species of plant life in 30 outdoor gardens and 10 greenhouses.

• **La Ronde Amusement Park,** Montreal: Contains the world's highest double-track roller coaster, giant water slides, an old-fashioned merry-go-round, an international circus, and more.

• **Montreal Museum of Fine Arts (MMFA),** Montreal: Founded in 1860, Canada's oldest museum houses a permanent collection of Canadian and European paintings, sculpture, and furnishings.

• **Museum of Contemporary Art,** Montreal: Performing arts events, cultural activities, traveling exhibitions, and a permanent collection of contemporary art by Québecois and international artists.

With more than 25,000 different species of plant life, Montreal's Botanical Gardens are the third largest in the world.

A prickly porcupine is one of the Quebec Zoological Gardens' more than 1,000 residents.

• **Quebec Zoological Gardens,** Quebec City: More than 1,000 specimens of more than 250 species of birds and several hundred mammals—especially native Canadian species—located on a 90-acre site.

• **Quebec Aquarium,** Quebec City: Features native and foreign saltwater fish, whales, dolphins, and other marine mammals and reptiles. Situated on a cliff overlooking the St. Lawrence River, it offers stunning views of Quebec City.

• **The Citadel,** Quebec City: The largest fort in North America still used as a military base, with a museum tracing Quebec's military history from the 17th to the 20th century. Featuring a daily Changing of the Guard.

• **Notre-Dame de Québec Basilica:** Quebec City: The headquarters of the Catholic church in Quebec.

• **Museum of Quebec,** Quebec City: An extensive permanent collection of painting, sculpture, and religious objects relating to the history of Quebec province.

• **Granby Zoo,** Granby: A 95-acre park with animals from all continents and a petting zoo for children.

• **Museum of Archaeology of the University of Quebec,** Trois Rivières: Comprehensive collection of fossils and artifacts from Indian and European settlements.

• **La Village Québecois d'Antan,** Drummondville: A reconstructed pioneer village, complete with costumed actors depicting life in a 19th-century Quebec community.

A costumed dancer participates in a parade during the town of Drummondville's annual World Folklore Festival.

Festivals

Snowmen amuse children during the world's largest winter carnival in Quebec.

Winter: The world's biggest **Winter Carnival** is Quebec City's answer to Mardi Gras: 10 days of ice sculpture competition, hockey tournaments, acrobatic skiing, dogsled racing, and a famous canoe race across the icy St. Lawrence River. Montreal hosts its own winter festival, **La Fête des Neiges.** Both winter festivals take place in late January or early February. Canada's favorite sport takes to the ice during Quebec City's **International Pee-Wee Hockey Tournament** for 10- to 13-year-olds.

Spring: Sample the province's delicious maple sugar products during the maple **Sugaring-Off** events in March in villages and towns in the Eastern Townships and the St. Lawrence Lowland. April finds book lovers at the **International Book Fair** at the Centre des Congrès de Quebec. In May, the **Benson & Hedges International Fireworks Competition** lights up Montreal's skies. Early June finds Montreal hosting the **Montreal International Music Competition,** while Quebec City's streets fill with jazz during **Les Nuits Bleues International des Jazz.** Later in the month, Montreal's world-class **International Jazz Festival** attracts thousands of jazz aficionados. June 24 is **La Fête National des Québecois,** Quebec's national festival, celebrated with parades, barbecues, and bonfires.

Summer: Quebec's **Summer Festival** takes place during the first two weeks in July with concerts and other special events. Comedy is the name of the game during Montreal's comedy festival, **Festival du Rire** (**"Just for Laughs"**). Montreal hosts the only competitive film festival recognized by the International Federation of Film Producers during the **Montreal World Film Festival.**

Fall: More than 10,000 runners compete in early September during Montreal's **International Marathon. Presence de Metiers d'Art de Québec** takes place in late November and features crafts by some 200 Quebec artists and artisans.

Chronology

1534   Jacques Cartier lands at Gaspé Peninsula and takes possession of the territory in the name of Francis I, King of France.

1535   Cartier sails to the Indian villages of Stadacona and Hochelaga, now Quebec and Montreal.

1608   Samuel de Champlain lands along the St. Lawrence River and establishes a settlement at Quebec City.

1642   Paul de Chomeday de Maisonneuve establishes a settlement at Ville-Marie de Montreal.

1663   Quebec becomes the capital of New France.

1759   British forces defeat the French at the Battle of the Plains of Abraham.

1763   Treaty of Paris signed, ending Seven Years' War between the French and British.

1774   The Quebec Act guarantees religious and linguistic freedom to Quebec.

1791   The Constitutional Act grants French Canadians their own homeland and divides Canada into two provinces, Upper and Lower Canada.

1841   The Union Act reunites Canada, proclaiming English as the official language.

1867   The British North America Act brings about the Canadian confederation of Quebec, Ontario, New Brunswick, and Nova Scotia.

1885   Canadian Pacific Railway completed, linking Quebec with the west.

1912   Quebec is enlarged to include part of the Northwest Territories.

1959   St. Lawrence Seaway completed.

1970   Health Insurance Act passed.

1974   French becomes Quebec's official language.

1977   Charter of the French Language makes French the official
         language of government and law. Minority rights to
         language and culture are respected and Indians living on
         reserved lands are exempt from charter provisions.

1979   First generators of the James Bay hydroelectric power
         project begin operation.

1980   A proposal by the Parti Québecois to make Quebec an
         independent nation is defeated in a popular referendum.

Hydroelectricity provides Quebec
with much of its energy requirements. This generator, at James
Bay, began operation in 1979.

Further Reading

Armitage, Peter. *The Inuit (Eskimo)*. New York: Chelsea House, 1990.

Butson, Thomas. *Pierre Elliot Trudeau*. New York: Chelsea House, 1986.

Boswell, Hazel. *French Canada: Pictures and Stories of Old Quebec*. New York: Atheneum, 1967.

Calloway, Colin. *The Abenaki*. New York: Chelsea House, 1989.

Ellenwood, Stephan E. *Quebec: Cultural Awareness*. Boston: Wide Horizons Discovery Program, 1980.

Fischler, Stanley I. *Montreal Canadiens*. Mankato, Minn.: Creative Education, 1986.

Graymont, Barbara. *The Iroquois*. New York: Chelsea House, 1988.

Griffin, Anne. *Quebec: The Challenge of Independence*. Rutherford, NJ: Fairleigh Dickinson University Press, 1984.

Hibbert, Christopher. *Wolfe at Quebec*. Cleveland: World, 1959.

Law, Kevin. *Canada*. New York: Chelsea House, 1990.

Lee, Susan. *Battle for Quebec*. Chicago: Childrens Press, 1973.

Levesque, René. *Memoirs*. Toronto: McClelland & Stewart, 1986.

McRoberts, Kenneth. *Quebec: Social Change and Political Crisis*. Toronto: McClelland & Stewart, 1986.

Neatby, Hilda Marion. *Quebec: The Revolutionary Age, 1760-1791*. Toronto: McClelland & Stewart, 1966.

Taner, Ogden. *The Canadians*. New York: Time-Life, 1977.

Tanobe, Miyuki. *Quebec, I Love You: Je t'Aime*. Plattsburgh, NY: Tundra, 1971.

Index

Photos pages 5, 9, 12, 13, 15, 32, 35, 36, 37, 41, 44, 46, 48, 49, 51, 53, 54, 58, and cover courtesy of Industry, Science and Technology Canada; pages 3, 8, 10, 11, 14, 16, 38, 39, 40, 42, 43, 45, 50, 56, 57, 59, and 61 courtesy of Québec Tourism; pages 18, 21, 23, 26, and 27 courtesy of the Bettman Archives; pages 29, 30, and 31 courtesy of UPI/Bettman Newsphotos; pages 19, 22, and 25 courtesy of the National Archives of Canada; drawings on page 7 by Debora Smith.

Suzanne LeVert is the author of four previous books for young readers. One of these, *The Sakharov File*, a biography of noted Russian physicist Andrei Sakharov, was selected as a Notable Book by the National Council for the Social Studies. Her other books include *AIDS: In Search of a Killer, The Doubleday Book of Famous Americans,* and *New York.* Ms. LeVert also has extensive experience as an editor, first in children's books at Simon & Schuster, then as associate editor at *Trialogue,* the magazine of the Trilateral Commission, and as senior editor at Save the Children, the international relief and development organization. She lives in Newburyport, Massachusetts.

George Sheppard, General Editor, is a lecturer on Canadian and American history at McMaster University in Hamilton, Ontario. Dr. Sheppard holds an honors B.A. and an M.A. in history from Laurentian University and earned his Ph.D. in Canadian history at McMaster. He has taught Canadian history at Nipissing University in North Bay. His research specialty is the War of 1812, and he has published articles in *Histoire sociale/Social History, Papers of the Bibliographical Society of Canada,* and *Ontario History.* Dr. Sheppard is a native of Timmins, Ontario.

Pierre Berton, Senior Consulting Editor, is the author of 34 books, including *The Mysterious North, Klondike, Great Canadians, The Last Spike, The Great Railway Illustrated, Hollywood's Canada, My Country: The Remarkable Past, The Wild Frontier, The Invasion of Canada, Why We Act Like Canadians, The Klondike Quest,* and *The Arctic Grail.* He has won three Governor General's Awards for creative nonfiction, two National Newspaper Awards, and two ACTRA "Nellies" for broadcasting. He is a Companion of the Order of Canada and a member of the Canadian News Hall of Fame and holds 12 honorary degrees. Raised in the Yukon, Mr. Berton began his newspaper career in Vancouver. He then became managing editor of *McLean's,* Canada's largest magazine, and subsequently worked for the Canadian Broadcasting Network and the *Toronto Star.* He lives in Kleinburg, Ontario.